JAN 3 0 2013

WITHDRAWN

W9-CHP-957

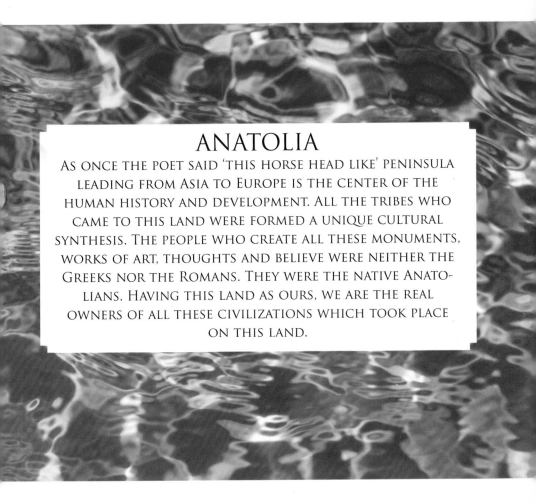

ANATOLIA

As once the poet said 'this horse head like' peninsula leading from Asia to Europe is the center of the human history and development. All the tribes who came to this land were formed a unique cultural synthesis. The people who create all these monuments, works of art, thoughts and believe were neither the Greeks nor the Romans. They were the native Anatolians. Having this land as ours, we are the real owners of all these civilizations which took place on this land.

LIBRARY

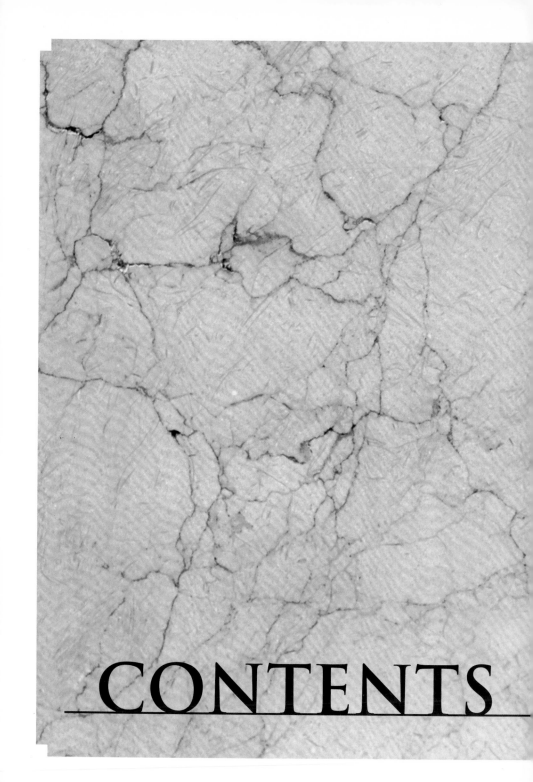

CONTENTS

THE HISTORY OF THE CITY AND ITS FOUNDATION

Hierapolis was a Hellenistic city which was founded at the upper plateau of the Lykos Valley between the Honaz (ancient Kadmos), Babadağ (ancient mountain Salbakos) and Çökelez Mountains. It took place at the center of the important trade routes during Antiquity. During the 3rd century B.C. it was one of the four colonies of Phrygia which was founded by the Seleucids. The others were Laodicea, Apameia and also Pisidian Antiocheia.

After the Alexander the Great, the region was ruled first under the Seleucid Dynasty (3rd century BC) and then in 190 BC under the Kingdom of Pergamum of which the ruler was Antiochus III who had the support of Romans.

Till this time Hierapolis was known as colonial city, after this date it was turned to a sacred city of which had a religious identity.

The chief god of the city was the god Apollo. He was called as 'Apollo Arche-getes' as the protector of the city; as 'Apollo Pythios' during the games and the festivals and as 'Apollo Kareios' for the oracle and for this reason a sacred area was established for him.

Hierapolis was ruled by the procouncils from 129 AD as a part of the Provincia Asia of the Roman Empire. The city was first included in the Kibra Conventes Union, and then to Pisidia Pacatiana during the 3rd century AD.

During the earliest years of the Roman Empire several tournaments and festi-vals were held in the city in the honour of the Emperor Augustus and gymnasium was built at the southern part of the city which was dedicated to Leto, Artemis and Apollo.

three beauties

The city was totally collapsed by the violent earthquakes two times during the years of 17th AD and the 60 AD and rebuilt again according to the Hippodamic (grid) plan. Especially under Emperor Domitianus (81-96AD) of the Roman Empire the monumental buildings were built in the city by Asian proconsul Julius Frontinus and were dedicated to the emperor.

In 129 AD, Emperor Hadrianus had visited the city and monumental agora had begun to be built with the money which was collected from the taxes. Emperor Hadrianus wrote two letters and the city had gained the opportunity of tax freedom, shelter and independence.

Hierapolis had lived its golden age during the 3rd century AD. Antipatros from Hierapolis was the teacher of the children of Emperor Septimius Severus; therefore the city got the benefits of the   emperor funds mostly.

It became one of the richest cities of Anatolia during 3rd century AD. A textile union was established among Hierapolis, Laodicea and Colossae, and the textile products were exported to Rome, to Egypt and also to all the eastern countries of the Roman Empire.

In Hierapolis, on one hand the pagan beliefs were continued, but on the other hand Christianity as a new religion was spread with the supports of the rich and the substantial Hebrew community. During the big earthquake in the 7th century AD., Hierapolis was ruined and the city was almost lost its identity. It turned to an agricultural city with the rural houses, and later in 12th century AD it turned to a small town. During 13th century AD the Seljuk Turks ruled over and the city was totally abandoned after an earthquake in the 14th century AD.

coronation of Hierapolis

The city has a general view over the Lykos Valley. The city was planned according to the Hippodamean-type plan (grid system). The streets had cut each other horizontally and diagonally, and the main street had two monumental gates at each end.

The water for drinking and usage were provided by two different sources and collected into a main reservoir. The water from here was distributed through the baked clay pipes which were lying below the streets, and the polluted waters were collected under the streets from where they were collected into main sewerage under the main street. From there polluted waters were taken to the dry springs which were on the Northern and the Southern outskirts of the city.

As the results of the excavations it was revealed that the underground facilities of the city were excellently designed and it also indicated that there are no signs of flood destruction in Hierapolis throughout the centuries in Antiquity.

In Hierapolis besides the agora which was an important trade center, there was also a second agora for the official works.

After the great earthquakes which took place at the years 17 and 60 AD., Hellenistic city of Hierapolis was built again having the characteristics of Roman city.

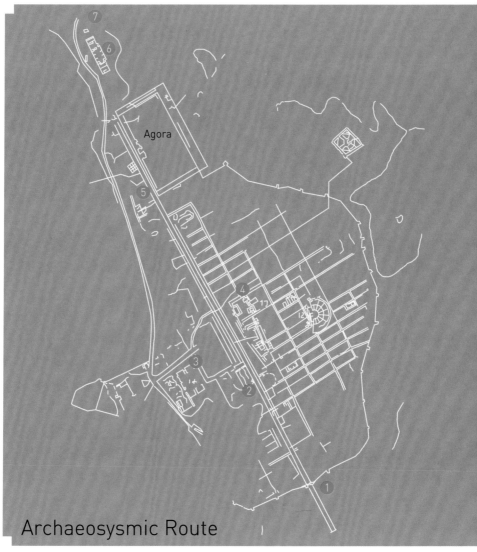

Agora

Archaeosysmic Route

1 South Byzantine Gate
2 Pier Church
3 Thermal Pool
4 Temple of Apollo
5 The Nymphaeum of the Tritons
6 Baths- Basilica Complex
7 Necropolis

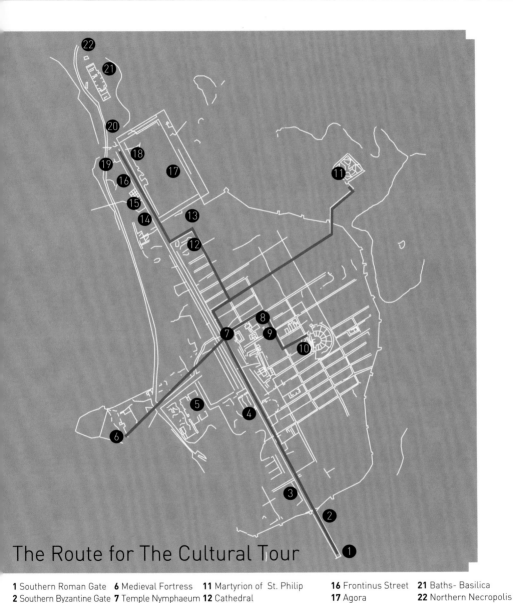

The Route for The Cultural Tour

1 Southern Roman Gate	**6** Medieval Fortress	**11** Martyrion of St. Philip	**16** Frontinus Street	**21** Baths- Basilica
2 Southern Byzantine Gate	**7** Temple Nymphaeum	**12** Cathedral	**17** Agora	**22** Northern Necropolis
3 Gymnasium	**8** Temple of Apollo	**13** Byzantine Bath	**18** Latrine	
4 Pier Church	**9** Plutonium	**14** The Nymphaeum of the Tritons	**19** The Workshop of Olive Oil	
5 Large Bath – Museum	**10** Theatre	**15** Northern Byzantine Gate	**20** Frontinus Gate	

THE EARTHQUAKES

The earthquakes which were known at Hierapolis took place during the 4th, 7th, 12th and 14th centuries AD., and at the years 17 and 60 AD. The city was totally collapsed during the earthquake in 60 AD, but later built again. After the earthquake during the 7th century AD, the city was turned to a provincial town whose economy was based on agriculture.

Nowadays the city is on the list of UNESCO's World Cultural Heritage. Besides its cultural and natural importance and the city has monuments which give important archeosysmic data to the international world. Amongst the buildings which were indicating the evidences of the earthquakes Agora, The Nymphaeum of the Tritons, Bath-Basilica and ancient pool can be mentioned.

The main street on the north-south direction, ca. 1 km. long, has divided the city into two parts. Two monumental gates took place at each end and it was also surrounded by the porticoes, public buildings, shops and the workshops.

THE SOUTHERN ROMAN GATE
The South Gate with its triple arch was dated to the same period with the North Gate and took place as the symmetrical of it. The middle arch was higher than the others. It was different from the North Gate because of its rectangular towers.

THE NORTHERN ROMAN GATE

The Northern Roman Gate was the main gate during the Roman Period. It took place at the end of the main street and it led form here towards to Laodicea and Colossai direction. According to the part of its inscription which was found on the later part of the wall, Frontinus was built not only the gate and the towers, but also the main road.

THE SOUTHERN BYZANTINE GATE
The Southern Byzantine Gate was built by the travertine blocks including some marble blocks and the spolie during the 5th century AD. As on the North Gate, it was flanked by two rectangular towers and a monolithic architrave with a relieving arch on it. However, the actual height of the door is somewhat lower than its twin.

THE NORTHERN BYZANTINE GATE
The Northern Byzantine Gate was built during the Theodosian reign at the 5th century AD as a part of the fortification system. Symmetrical of the south gate, it was also the main gate during the Byzantine Period.

THE GYMNASIUM

The Gymnasium was built under the reign of Emperor Augustus and was one of the most important buildings of the city. It was used for the cultural activities and for the physical education of the citizens. According to the inscription on it, it was dedicated to Leto, Artemis and Apollo.

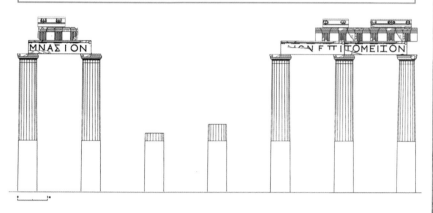

THE TEMPLE OF APOLLO AND THE CENTER OF ORACLE

The temple of Apollo and Oracle Center were established on the old Plutonium grotto which had a religious importance. This place was also the cult center of the local people and dedicated to the mother goddess Cybele. Here Apollo and Cybele were met together. According to the ancient writers; the priests of Cybele were not affected from the poisonous gases in the grotto.

The ruins of the upper structure of Apollo Temple and the Oracle Center were dated back to the 3rd century AD. not before. To the sacred area one could only reach by the broad stairs. The sacred place was encircled by a temenos wall. In the middle of the oracle center a bothros took place. Also, a monumental nymphaeum with a U-design was built on the columned street side during the 4th century AD.

On an inscription which was found at the sacred area, the oracle of the god Apollo was written by 24 Greek letters in an alphabetic order. The beginning of each verse corresponded to one of the letters of the Greek alphabet. During Antiquity the citizens were not allowed to enter the sacred area. To consult the oracle, a person first must give a sacrifice and than take any letter from the tripot and gave this letter to the priest. Then the priest would answer the queries according to the letter that was given to him as the god was answering.

Plutonium which took place at the bottom of the Oracle Center had a different kind of importance and according to pagan belief it was known as the passing gate of Hades to the Under

world. At the entrance of the gate there was a beautiful marble niche and three stairs descending to the downstairs to the underworld. Plutonium was an interesting place because of the fault line which caused poisonous gases and vast amount of spring waters.

According to the ancient belief, the soul of the dead would be tranquillized when they reached to the world of Hades. The dead were taken by the ferryman Charon, whose fee for this service was placed in the mouth of the corpse. During the excavations the coins were found in the mouth of the corpse. Plutonium was the main and the most important passage gate to the Underworld, the world of Hades. Therefore, Hierapolis was accepted as a sacred city during Antiquity Era. Many inscriptions from the different temples of the many cities all around the Anatolia displayed the rivalry between the priests and the city council members because of the income from the skins of sacrificed animals.

THEATRE

The theatre was a large building in a Greek theatre type, 300 feet wide, was protected with almost all of its architectural elements and with its cavea leaning against the slope of a hill. The first building phase built at the travertine blocks and has a small scaenae dated to the 1st century AD. It was damaged during the earthquake in 60 AD, and the reconstruction was begun during Flavians. It was still under construction during the Hadrianic Age (117-138 AD) and was finished during the Severians (206 AD).

Its cavea has 50 seating rows and was divided 7 parts with 8 stairs. Diazoma took place in the middle of the cavea. Vaulted passages led to **Vomitorium** which were on both sides. In the middle there was the box of the administrator and the orchestra which was surrounded by the front walls of the stage. The wall was 3.66 m. high having 5 doors and 6 niches. In front of them 10 marble columns took place. The seashell motives were carved on the top of the columns. On the walls behind the stage there were 3 different rows of columns. The lower row of the columns had octagonal bases. Amongst the columns there were the sculptors of the four goddesses such as Hera, Aphrodite, Demeter and Persephone.

The Ruins of Hierapolis from the Theatre

On the west part of the theatre there was a latrine (public toilettes). The friezes in the theatre had depicted the mythological scenes such as the birth of Apollo and Artemis; the ritual scenes; the processions of Dionysos, Satry and the Maenads; the music contest between Apollo and Marsyas; the battle between the gods and the giants; the abduction of Persephone by Hades to the Underworld; and also several festivals which were held in Hierapolis and the coronation of Emperor Septimius Severus who had supported the restoration of the theatre. The friezes of Hierapolis had a close resemblance to the friezes of theatres of Perge, Side and Nysa.

BATHS-BASILICA

Bath Basilica complex was located on the north side of the city, out of the city gates. The bath was dated to the 3rd century AD, but later in 6th century AD an apse was added to the central part and it was turned into a church. The back wall of the building was leaned during an earthquake. The consolidation works are continuing to protect this wall with all the traces of the earthquake.

In ancient times to purification and cleaning before entering the city was a common tradition in Anatolia, or they would not accepted to the city. Therefore, the bath buildings were generally located at the outskirts of the city. This was an important sign of sensitivity of ancient Anatolian people about the cleaning and protecting against epidemics.

29

LATRINE (PUBLIC TOILETTES)

The latrine took place at the beginning of the main street. It was divided by two rows of Doric monolithic columns which had supported the heavy entablature built by the travertine blocks. A drain was established under the building and was linked to the sewerage system on the main street. The polluted waters were thrown from here. A sitting bench with the holes took place along the perimeter wall. In front to the channel which carried the polluted water another channel was built for carrying clean running water for hygienic usage. The pavement was covered by the travertine slabs. On the account of monumentality, these kinds of buildings were as important as the other monumental buildings of the road. Besides the bath buildings and the nymphaeums, latrines were the sign of prestige for the city. It was the indication of cleaning services of the city for the people.

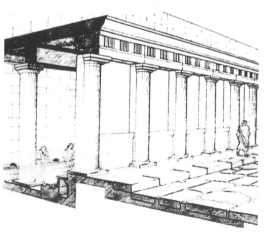

Before the earthquake of 60 AD, the suburban areas were used as agora for the necropolis and the workshops. After the earthquake a new vast area between the Frontinus Street and the slopes of the eastern hill was organized as the commercial agora of Hierapolis. Having the circular kilns in these workshops many Megarian Wares with relief decoration, dated to the 1st century BC were found.

During the 2nd century AD, a new agora was built, in this area 170 m. in width and 280 m in length, which was one of the largest agora in Asia Minor. The most popular gladiator combats were held in the center of it.

HOUSES

On the eastern slopes of the city were the areas for the houses of the citizens. During the excavations many houses and house complexes were revealed like the slope houses of Ephesus. The houses with the atriums decorated with the frescoes and mosaics have been found. The most remarkable part of this area was the house with its praying room. All the walls were decorated with the frescoes and the pray of Solomon from the Bible in Latin were written on the wall. The excavations are still in progress on the area of the 'The House of the Ionic Capitals' near the theatre, for the understanding of the social life and to reveal the architectural aspects of the houses.

THE WORKSHOP OF OLIVE OIL

The workshop was established in four parts to process the olives.

• An elliptic pool to work as the first step on olives, or to wash the olives after collecting.

• A pressing stone with a hole and a beam of it which was lost nowadays

• A stone ground established by the thick stones for the processing of the olives which were collected in the baskets.

• A large baked clay pithos for collecting the oil of the pressed olives

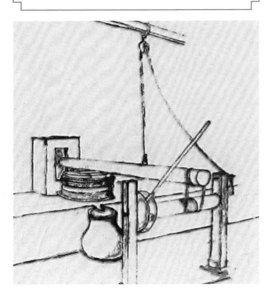

THE NYMPHAEUM OF THE TRITONS

According to the demands of the citizens, the monumental nymphaeums were built in order to give beauty to the city. They were amongst the public buildings. The Hierapolis Nymphaeum was built at the end of the 3rd and the beginning of the 4th century AD on the main street. It was one of the most monumental fountains amongst the others in Asia Minor. It was building on the main street, was two stories high and on the pediments the Amazon warriors and the tritons playing trumpets were depicted.

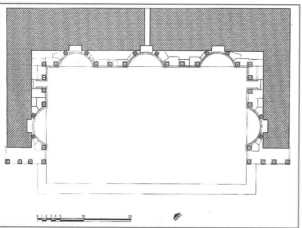

THE CATHEDRAL

The cathedral which was dated back at the beginning of the 6th century AD. had a door on the right hand side that opened to the baptismal fond and with the nartex and the atrium it opened to the main street. It had a rectangular plan and was divided by columns to three naves. The circular baptismal font, having steps on two sides and which were revetted with marble, was discovered in the apsidal area. The entablature where the women's department took place was carried by columns that were second in the row. Interior of the apse had of circular plan and on the outside it was polygonal. The interior of the main apse was occupied by the 'Synthronon', the stepped semicircular benches that were reserved for the clergy and the bishop during the lithurgy.

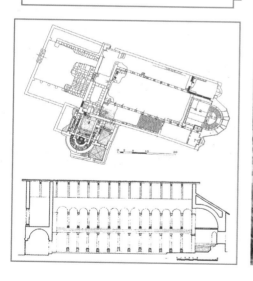

THE CHURCH WITH PIERS

The building with a nave and two aisles was preceded by a portico with piers. This was not seen in other cathedrals and churches. The sizes of the piers were different from each other. It was an unusual feature and resembled the traditional Roman building technique. The piers divided the central space into four bays. This section given to priests had a pseudo-transept plan.

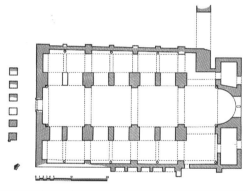

THE MARTYRION OF ST. PHILIP

St. Philipp was one of the twelve saints of Jesus, and was murdered while he was trying to spread Christianity in 80 AD during his visit to Hierapolis with his two daughters. When Christianity was accepted as an official religion in 5th century AD, 'Martyrion' was built in name to his honour on the eastern hill, out of the city walls. Later on the city walls were united with long stair to this building. In front of the stairs an octagonal planned bath building and besides to it a fountain 'Haghiasma' took place.

seal lead-mail

Martryrion was a remarkable building with the dimensions of 20X20m. having octagonal plan. The building was capped by a wooden dome covered with lead supported by eight pillars. The two façades both had porticos. At the center of the building there was the marble tomb of the Martry. The halls were decorated with the mosaics. The pavements of the front rooms were covered with the travertine slabs. The pavements of the outer rooms in which the pilgrims were living were also covered with pressed soil. The building had eight chapels.

The central part of the building was used as a meeting room in which the legends were told about the life of St. Philip, his duties and the torture he faced while spreading Christianity. The building was also used for a pilgrimage, as well as the spiritual healing center.

MARBLE PORTICO

The portico, 60 m. in length and app. 5.5 m. in height were opened to the main street. The back all was constructed with marble blocks and was decorated with columns. At the corner of the façade there was a pillar continuing with the row of Doric styled marble columns. There was a dedicatory inscription on the architrave.

This monument was probably collapsed in the earthquake of the 4.th century AD. and the ruins were buried under the deposit. Later calcareous water coming from the hill left its sediment which covered the whole area.

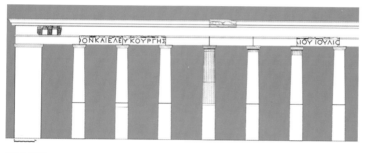

We learn much about the city of Hierapolis from the inscriptions and coins. The administrative system of Hierapolis was the same as in the other cities of Asia Minor. The people were represented and administrated by Demos. From the reign of Emperor Carracalla onwards the administration of the city was done by the people selected by the corporations.

On the coins the portraits of the priestess carrying the crowns with laurel leaves on their heads as well as the personification of Demos as a youth, carrying the leadership crown were depicted (this represented the Boule, the City Hall).

The foremost citizens of the city were chosen for the leadership and membership. High officials and the military commandants were also taken part in the administration of the city. The finance officials of the city were controlled the treasury and collected the taxes with the help of special commissions. A large group of the citizens were taken place as the administrators. They were administrating the agricultural works, gymnasia and Gerusia. They were also became ambassadors to other cities. The most important corporation of the city was Gerusia (council of elderly people).

Hierapolis was administrated by the proconsul in the name of the Emperor. The main population of the city were the natives of Asia Minor, where as Greeks, Romans and Jewish people were also took an important part in the population.

The Asia Minor natives, known as Phrygians coming from the same race with the god Apollo who was at the same time, the chief god of the city usually carry the names given by Apollo. Several inscriptions had bared these names. They also had continued to live their traditional cults such as Cybele-Attis cult.

The Romans were usually the merchants and their population increased within the years. Their shops were located on the main street. The high trade potential of the city were attracted the merchants from the nearby cities such as Aphrodisias and Sardes.

The substantial families of Hierapolis were Zeuxdemus, Avgustos Zenon and sophist Antipater. Antipater was a well known citizen of Hierapolis. He was born in 150-160 AD, and educated at the sophistical school and had lectures from the famous philosophers and scholars of Athens. He was chosen by Emperor Septimius Severus as a teacher for his sons Carrracalla and Geta. He also had a degree as a council from the emperor. Most probably he died and buried in his family tomb in Hierapolis.

The valley of Lykos was very fertile in growing up and cultivating every kind of crops. The spring waters were used for the irrigation of the agricultural lands. Using the channels, the water was brought from the hills.

Besides the textile industry, leather, marble trading, sheep breeding, wool production and dyeing of textiles were the most important sources of income. Hierapolis was famous for the herds of sheep. Therefore, the union of animal breeders, the union of dyers, and the union of wool producers had gained a great influence in the city. The industry of Hierapolis was based on the wool. The wool was produced by the city itself. Therefore, Hierapolis was like a factory city of Asia Minor during Antiquity.

graphic reconstroction of a hydraulic saw represented on the sarcophagus.

THE CITY OF THE DEADS (NECROPOLIS)

During burial ceremony coins were put into the mouth of the deceased for ferryman Charon whom he thought to be the man taking them to the Underworld. As well as the mouths, they also put money in the palm of the hands for afterlife. The symbols and reliefs on the tombs were the signs of the identity of the dead. Amongst them a Jewish tomb with Menorah; a tomb of a leather merchant with a symbol of leather; and a tomb of gladiator with the reliefs of a shield, a sword, a trident and an amphora on it can be mentioned. On many tombs the curse texts were written in order to forbid people from touching them. In one example, the owner of the tomb had wanted not to close the scenery of his tomb.

In the tombs with the temple plan, the big stone slabs were established on the roof according to the brick style in order to protect the grave from the rain. When the tombs were used for the multi burials, the former skeletons were collected and taken to the craters under the klinai or in the urns , like in the Jewish Tomb. Belonging to the Roman Period, the upper structure of the tombs was mostly the false tombs, where the grave chamber was placed under the ground level. In a catacomb style tomb, it was found that the bones and the ashes were put into the urns and the craters in the 24 different niches. This indicates that the cremation burials were among the burial tradition in Hierapolis. Since Hierapolis was accepted as a sacred city having shortage of land, the remains of the former burials were cremated in order to open new places for the burials and the tombs which were emptied were used by the same families for centuries.

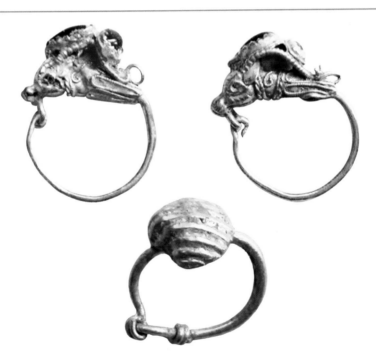

THE CITY OF THE DEADS (NECROPOLIS)

After the funeral as a tradition, three different days in that month, the whole family and the friends were collected together for his remembrance of the dead, having funeral feast and praying.   East, North and South parts of the city there were necropolises. Since Hierapolis was accepted as a sacred city and also having a healing center, the people from the nearby cities were demanded to be buried here, especially when they have died after an illness. The necropolises of Hierapolis were very important for showing the wealth and comfort of the people living in the city.

The Lamps: The lamps in which the olive oil and animal oils were burned were used for the illumination. They were among the most important objects of the religious ceremonies since earlier times. Many of them were dedicated to the gods. They were also used to illuminate the offerings to the graves them and the souls of the dead. Since they were accepted by many people as a symbol of happiness, ancient people used to believe in not to extinguish the lamps.

TUMULUS NR. 51 [1ST CENTURY BC]

This tumulus was built by the travertine blocks, had a circular plan and covered with a conical earth dome. Beside the walls, there were two step stairs that led the burial chamber in which there were funerary beds. The door of the chamber was closed by a stone plate. The tomb was built during the Late Hellenistic period. It was dated back to the 1st century AD according to the inscription, bearing the name of Lucius Salvius Paolinus.

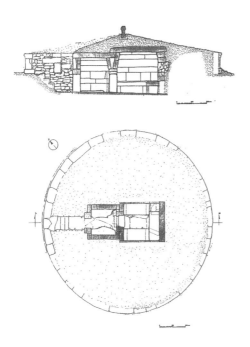

This tomb was located near the monumental entrance gate. It was built on a stepped platform surrounded by a bench. The tomb was flanked by two half columns at the corners and had a Doric trighylp-metop friese decorated with the rosettes on it. On the upper part of it the inscription relating the activities of the merchant Titus Flavius Zeuxis were recorded. He had to pass Cape Malea for 72 times in order to go to Italy. Below the pedestal, the stairs lead was leading down to the burial chamber which was carved into the calcareous rock. There were three funeral beds inside the burial chamber. This area was also encircled by a wall constructed with the small stones and the sarcophagi inside was belonged to the members of the same family.

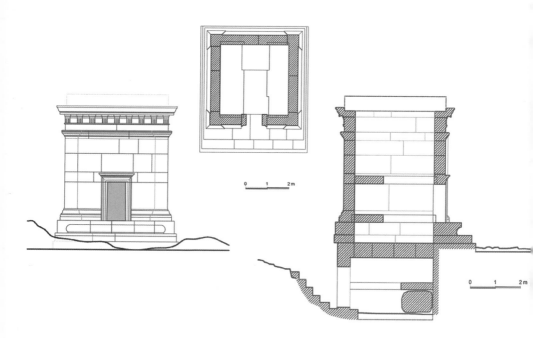

THE TOMB NR 114 [SECOND HALF OF THE 2ND CENTURY AD]

The tomb was located at the left side of the northern necropolis within a circuit wall. It was raised on a three stepped platform and had a sitting row in front. In the burial chamber there were three funerary beds and an ossuary. The sarcophagus on the tomb was belonged to Aelius Apollinarius and his wife Neratia Apollinis. It was damaged during an earthquake. An interesting inscription on the façade recorded the curses and the punishments against the people who would damage the tomb. According to the inscription besides the monetary punishments, the punishments of the infernal gods would be given to the person whoever would behave out of the orders. Therefore, the tomb was also known as 'The Tomb of the Cursed'.

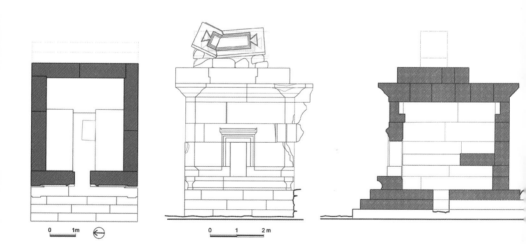

This tomb had an interesting façade, resembling to the house architecture because of its windows. The entrance door of the area had a molded architrave. It had also a backyard in which two sarcoghagi took place. Also with two stairs one could enter to the other burial chambers that were covered by barrel vaults.

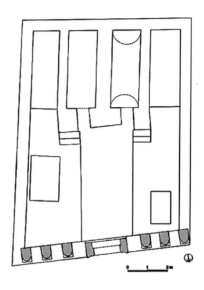

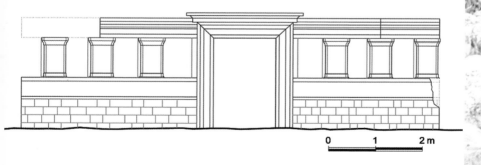

THE TOMB OF THE GLADIATORS [2ND-3RD CENTURY AD]

The tomb took its name from the reliefs depicting the fighting gladiators (from the left: an amphora filled with oil which was a present for the winner; a trident and a short sword which symbolized the fight and a shield with the emblem of showing the school of the gladiator). The building had two building phase. It was first built as a rectangular building and with the funeral beds on the walls. Then a new façade was added which was connected with the entrance. The short edges were also supported in order to bear the sarcophagi that were put on them.

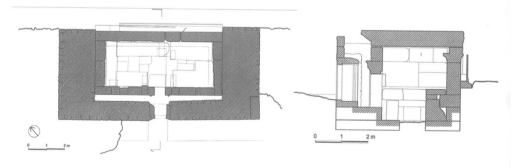

This tomb was belonged to a Jewish family. It had an elaborated façade, a gate decorated with the moldings and a gabled roof. Under a burial chamber with rectangular shape which took place on a high podium on the travertine rocks, an untouched burial chamber was discovered having thirty-one skeletons . Among the findings in the middle part of it, there were two urns and a crater in which the bones of the former burials, and at the door entrance there was a silver amulet with its protection cover. On the amulet there were writings in old Greek about the protection against the injuries.

The chief god of the city was Apollo, but the old cult of Cybele (later Leto) was also continued. The local citizens were continued to adore Cybele (especially to the cult of Cybele-Attis) .Here the cults of Apollo Lermenos, Apollo Kareos and Apollo Archegetes were united together. Leto, Dionysos, Hades, Demeter, Aphrodite, Artemis and Athena were among the other gods and the goddesses of the city and they were depicted on the reliefs of the theater. Later during the Roman period, Imperial Cult had gained importance.

The Mythological Scenes on the Reliefs of the Theatre

Dionysos Festivals

Dionysos was the god of the grapes, wine and the mystic ecstasy. He had an Anatolian origin and it was believed that the wine leaf was first taken to this land by him. He was depicted in a drunken position with his fellows, the Satrys and the Maenads, accompanied by the centaurs and Erotes during Dionysiac festivals. The first theatre plays were written and played at the stage during the Dionysos Festivals in the name to honour him.

The Birth of Apollo and Artemis

According to the mythology, Leto, pregnant from Zeus, because she was afraid of Hera had given birth to Apollo at Patara in Lycia and Artemis in Claros near to the town of Selçuk. On the relief, Leto was depicted on a bed while giving birth to Apollo with the help of the servants. During the sacred birth of Artemis, the young girls were watching with the lavender branches and poppies in their hands.

The Group of Apollo-Marsyas

Goddess Athena made a flute from the reeds for herself. When she noticed that she was getting ugly while playing the flute, had thrown away the musical instrument. Marsyas had found the flute and played so beautifully that gained the aspiration of the nymphs. When Apollo the God of Music heard about the Marsyas flute playing he had organized a music contest and he had chosen King Midas as a judge. At the end of the contest God Apollo was naturally chosen because he was a God. But Midas did not accept this verdict. He chose Marsyas as the winner. Apollo got very angry to this and had turned the ears of Midas to the ears of an ass. He also punished Marsyas who had entered the contest with him. He flayed him alive. The nymphs of the water and the meadows who used to listen to the flute of Marsyas were very sad about it. Later, Apollo was also felt sorry for what he had done, had turned Marsyas to Çine Stream. The sound of the water in the stream resembled the music of Marsyas.

The Niobids Group

The story of Niobe was derived from an Anatolian legend. She was born at Sipylos (Manisa) Mountain where her father was the King. She was grown up with goddess Leto, and they were close friends. Niobe was married with Amphion, the King of Thebai and gave birth to twelve children, six boys, six daughters. But Leto has only two. She was proud of her twelve children, and saw herself in a better position than Leto. When Apollo and Artemis saw the sorrow of their mother, they killed all the children of Niobe with their bows and arrows. Niobe had turned into a stone because of her disaster. Today the rock mass in Manisa resembling a face of a woman was called as the 'weeping rock' and it thought to represent Niobe.

Persephone's Abduction by Hades

Persephone was the daughter of Zeus and Demeter who was the goddess of nature and fertility. According to the story, one day while picking flowers Hades suddenly came from the Underworld with his quadriga and abducted her to underground. Demeter had sought her daughter everywhere, but could not able find her. The God of Sun who had witnessed the incident told Demeter the place of her daughter. Being very angry, Demeter had damaged the nature. The earth got drought, famine began and all the seasons were turned into winter. The gods all came together under the leadership of Zeus and reached a conclusion. Zeus later ordered Hades to turn Persephone to her mother. Persephone was thus obliged to spend a half of each year with Hades and the other half with her mother. The return of Persephone to earth was accepted as the beginning of the spring. This legend about the formation of seasons had lived from very early dates under different names.

The Myth of Adonis

Adonis was emerged from the body of a myrrh tree. He was one of the most handsome youth among the mortals. Aphrodite has fallen in love with him and entrusted him to Persephone in order to hide him. Unfortunately, Persephone too has fallen in love with him and she did not want to give him back to Aphrodite. An argument took place between two goddesses. Meantime, Adonis was fatally injured during a wild boar hunting and died. Later the goddess Aphrodite begged Zeus to give him back.

Giganthomachia
This was the battle between the gods and the giants. All the Olympian gods took place in this battle. In this relief, Apollo was seen as killing the son of Mother Ge with his arrow and also goddess Athena were depicted.

THE GLADIATORS

The word gladiator came from the word 'gladus', which meant 'sword' in Latin. As seen in the Early Etruscan works of art, the sword was used during the first gladiator combats. Gladiator games originally came from Etruscan tradition, but the first games were held at Rome in 264 BC. The Senate of Rome was officially accepting these games in 105 BC. and then these games were held in Syria, Asia Minor and Egypt. The slaves were trained in the gladiator schools and took place in the combats. This education was accepted during the 1st century AD in Asia Minor and many buildings were constructed for these games. Many organizations about these games were arranged and staged. Spartacus of Thracia was the most popular gladiator of all times.

"may it be a good omen"
Beginning of II. rd. century A.D. Hierapolis, Northern Necropolis this monument belongs to the leader of the "venationes" group, Gnaeus Arrius Apuleius Aurellianus and was built by his Tribune son and wife named Aurelia Melitine Atticiana.

memorial inscriptions

In Hierapolis in the light of the inscriptions and the findings it was known that there were many gladiator schools with the shows that were very popular among the people. Agora was used for this kind of shows. The two necropolises of gladiators at the Northern Necropolis and on Tripolis Street were also very important. An inscription and the panel reliefs, were found in one of the necropolis; a shield decorated with a rosette, short sword, a trident and an amphora relief was found in the other. Amphora was given to the winning school. In Hierapolis the money and a Black Figured amphora full of olive oil were given to the winners as a reward.

In the museum on a gravestone of gladiator, the figure of the dead gladiator and six wreaths were depicted. The wreaths were the signs of the glory.

The most popular games in Hierapolis were 'Apollo Pytheos Games' which were the games dedicated on behalf of the city god Apollo. From the coins and inscriptions, it was understood that the most important festivals were dedicated to Apollo Archeytes and Dionysos. The musicians who took place at these games were also very popular among the people. The money was given to the winners and their statues were put in the agora. The people from nearby cities were also participated in these festivals. Hierapolis had earned a great amount of money from these festivals.

The coins printed on the behalf of these festivals the head of Apollo Lermenos was depicted, as well as the gods and the goddesses of the cities which were participated in the festivals. This was mostly seen on the coins of Ephesus. Ephesus was the harbour city for the merchants of Hierapolis. The importance of Ephesus came from its geographical position as a harbour city. On these anonymous coins, Artemis Ephesia was frequently depicted.

MUSEUM-ROMAN BATH

The bath building in Hierapolis was located at the centre of the city as a building complex. The departments were the palaestra, the library and the bath. In the unexcavated front part of the building it was thought that there was a market place as at many bath complexes in Asia Minor.

At the centre of palaestra a marble swimming pool takes place. Palaestra was used for the sporting activities during the Antiquity. The bath was heated by the hypocaust system, and the walls of the sudatorium (sweating room) were heated by the steam of water. The rooms inside the building were arranged according to a system: first the room with cold water pool, then tepidarium, laconicum (the lukewarm water room), sudatorium (sweating room), caldarium (hottest room) and before dressing entering again into the cold water. After the bath, the young people had their lessons with their instructors at the open air terraces or at the library. During the Antiquity these cult buildings were used as training and education. The three rooms of the bath were restored and were turned into the Archaeological Museum. Different objects coming from different historical places around Denizli were displayed in here.

CENTRAL BATH

The bath complex which was thought to be build during the 2nd.century AD, took place at the center of the city where the hot springs were gathered. It was built by travertine blocks and covered the area of 1.5 hectares, having the dimensions of 140X100 meters. The entrance to the building was through the Room A, leading to the main room 20x32 meters in dimension, covered with cradle vault having three exedras which were decorated with stucco and the walls were covered by colourful marble blocks.

The rooms C and D were interpreted as caldarium. The wide area on the east was covered by the rectangular rooms (L,M,N,O) having the functions of palaestra. They were opened to a courtyard having columns on the front side which were built by the local breccia.

After an earthquake which took place in the second half of the 4th century AD, the ceiling of the room H was covered by a new barrel vault and the two long sides were decorated with the marble columns from Apollo Temple.

Triton : The sculpture of triton which was found in the theatre, was depicted as half human and half fish since he was the son of Poseidon God of Sea and Amphitrite. During the 4th century AD the part of orchestra in the theatre was used as a place for the water games.

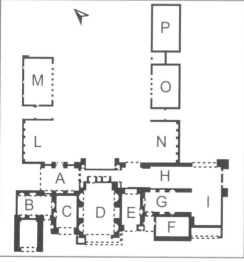

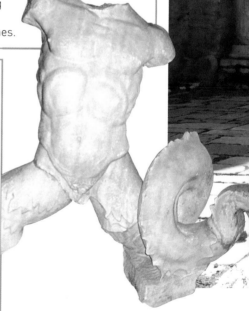

The sculpture of Phrygian god Attis was found during the excavation of the western part of the Agora. It was dated to the end of 2nd century AD. It was related to the local cult of Cybele in Hierapolis. According to the myth he was so handsome that he was passionately loved by Cybele. Attis however, could not reject the love he felt to Nymph Sagaritis, who was the ferry of the river Sangarius. Cybele in her rage cut the tree to which the life of Nymph was closely bounded .Learning the death of his lover he castrated himself From the blood he had lost, violets grew. Being sorry for what she had done, Cybele turned Attis to a pine tree. Because of this reason all the priests of Cybele were castrated. In the name of Cybele and Attis, May Festivals began to be organized. The painted sculpture with long curly hair having traces of color on were described as having a local dress, a long Phrygian cap and a pair of Phrygian shoes.

MEDICAL OFFICAL

The sculpture of a high ranked medical official was found besides all the other sculptures of the gods and the goddesses in the theatre. Near her leg there was found garlic, a louse comb and a mortar. This is very important from the view of the great value given to woman of Anatolia during the Antiquity.

HADES

Hades, the god of Underworld was the son of Chronos and the brother of Zeus and Poseidon. He had droved from the Underworld just once and abducted Persephone, daughter of Demeter. He was depicted as bearded like his brother Zeus. He had sat on a throne and near him were an eagle and Cerberus, the dog of hell. He was the owner of all the treasures of the Underworld. Therefore, the Romans called him 'Pluto' meaning 'the Rich'.

LETO

The sculpture of Leto was also found at the theatre. She was one of the native mother goddess of Anatolia. She gave birth to Apollo and Artemis after having relationship with Zeus.

APOLLO KAREIOS

The cult of Apollo Kareios was a local cult and related with the oracle of Apollo. The sculpture was found at the theatre, depicted in a soldier garment which is a rare depiction. There was an inscription at the pediment. Many inscriptions indicated that the adornment and purification at the Temple of Apollo Lermenos were done by god Apollon himself.

An altar which was previously built for the goddess Cybele later turned to a place of adornments to god Apollo on a hill overlooking the Valley of Maiandros. This was the center where people had came for purification from their sins.

The marble and travertine pieces of a frontal pediment had belonged to a small temple found at an olive grove at Develi Village near Pamukkale. At the middle of the pediment Persephone depicted as deriving from the acanthus. Arrow throwing three Erotes and three Graces take place on its two sides. This was an important example indicating the cult of Demeter-Persephone in Hierapolis.

THE SARCOPHAGUS OF LAODICEA

It was built by a Laodicean workshop between the 2nd-3rd centuries AD. It was belonged to an archon from the city of Laodicea. The figures of the man and his wife took place on its lid. The reliefs on the four sides depicted how an ideal administra

tor must have been. In order to be an ideal administrator one should have wisdom, in good relationships with gods, be a good hunter and warrior.

ANCIENT POOL

The ancient pool took place at the centre on the public Agora of Hierapolis. After an earthquake during the 7th century AD, the fault was formed where the spring water came out. An Ionic portico in it was the remains after the earthquake. This is the most popular thermal pool in Hierapolis for the visitors from all over the world. It is also an important health place and the visitors win their health back at this pool.

THERMAL WATERS AND THE TRAVERTINES OF PAMUKKALE

The most important reason for the construction of the city at this place was the sources of thermal waters. The place was important during Antiquity. The sacred spring waters beyond Plutonium, the cult center of Apollo, three water tanks, and the pools were among the attractive points in this area. The newly excavated tholos building at the middle of the first pool carry the traces of libation with the sacred waters. A long inscription for the honour of Zeuxidemos found here were relating to the organizations of the gladiator and wild animal games and the building activities he had sponsored. In addition, two inscriptions were found which were sent by Emperor Antonius Pius from Naples to the honour of Zeuxidemos.

The word 'travertine' came from the Roman city Tivertino (Tivoli) where deposits of travertine were found place. Travertine is a kind of multi-shaped rock which was formed by precipitation and showed different characters depending on the changes in conditions and factors.

THERMAL WATERS AND THE TRAVERTINES OF PAMUKKALE

The transformation of hot spring into normal conditions results in the precipitation and the formations of travertine. The excessive amount of calcium bicarbonate in hot spring and the carbon dioxide come out when water reaches to the surface and thus the calcium carbonate precipitates. Meanwhile, molecule water forms.

The analysis carried out at the source show that the amount of carbon dioxide in the spring is app.725mg/l, while this amount decreases to 145mg/l when water leaves

the travertine. According to the results of this analysis, out of 1 lt.water, 499,9mg CaCo precipitates on the travertine. That means 43191 gr. precipitation occurs out of 1 lt.water in a day. The travertine of which the average density is 1.48 gr/cm^3, its precipitation volume comprises an area of 29.2 dm^3. Depending on this theoretical approach, 2,4km^2 field/ area with the thickness of 2mm. can be whitened.

In ancient times the people were always eager to learn their future. They were used to attend the priest and the magicians as it happens nowadays. The most important oracle places of the ancient world were Delphoi, Didyma and Claros. The uncertain answers were sending from God by the help of the priests and the priestess. In Hierapolis it was believed that the god gave the answers in a written form. The oracle was belonged to Apollo Kareios which was intersected with the local cults. Anyone who wanted to learn the future must give a sacrifice to the temple than take a letter amongst 24 letters of the Greek alphabet from the tripot of Apollo. Then the priest would read the line opposite to the letter given as the god himself.

A The god himself will sort out for the things you are anxious about

B The venerable Tyche accepts the good decisions

Γ Farmer, as they say, take a snake into his bossom

Δ Run away from the things that should be feared, inspect carefully before doing anything

E As Nemesis is propitious, have faith in you actions

Z Life has its own times : why, man, are you needlessly anxious?

H Nemesis shakes the scales of justice for mortals

Θ Resolutely take action and conclude it

I Apollo who holds the glorious bow will give you strenght in your feats

K It is difficult to combat the waves: bide your time

Λ Take, share and thus receive joy

M You are proceeding in vain, don't hurry, its pointless

N From the tenebrous night once appeared a luminous ray

Ξ External advice will guide you better

O Sour grapes, if you wait, will mature in their own time

Π The slow tortoises precede the crows, even if they are winged

P Don't try, if you sail alone, to oppose the currents

Σ The King of the Immortals will save you with the oracles of Kareios

T Why are you so hurry ? If you wait you can go with greater happiness

Y If there is still time, later there will be nothing suspect

Φ Escape from friends that are worth little and trust the best

X The god that looks after you will bring you an unexpected joy

Ψ Know that purification of soul and body is arriving

Ω To whoever the god is favourable, Kareios concedes fortune

The aim of the integration plan is to protect all the natural and archaeological values of the travertine, the sources of the thermal waters and the ruins from corrosion and the destruction given to them people who come and visit.

After the international meetings and investigations this plan was revealed. The main target of this plan is to remove the hotels and the other buildings that were built between 1950 and 1960 for developing of tourism in this area. The other aim is to construct a new water distribution system in order to give fresh water to the travertines.

According to this plan, entering to the site by the vehicles was forbidden. The people leave their vehicles at the parking area of the entrance gates that are built in the North and the South of Pamukkale. The application of this plan was put into work, and a balance between protection archaeological and natural Pamukkale site and usage of this area was established.

All the buildings in the site were pulled down and the green areas and the viewing terraces were built in their places. All Pamukkale is surrounded by wire fence and in passing points the controls are done electronically.

According to the 'The Water Distribution and the Whitening Plan' prepared by Hacettepe University, the travertines of Pamukkale were divided into seven parts and to each part fresh waters are given. The whole area is controlled by the mobese cameras. The natural and archaeological site of Pamukkale is under the control of Directorate of Pamukkale Administration which was established by the governor of Denizli.

BIBLIOGRAPHY

Fede Berti, Daria De Bernardi Ferrero, Aslantepe, Hierapolis, Iasos, Kyme, Marsilio, 1995.

Francesco D'Andria and Francesca Silvestrelli, Lycos Vadisi Türk Arkeoloji Araştırmaları (The Turkish Researches at Lycos Valley), 2000.

Francesco D'Andria and M. Piera Caggia, Hierapolis Di Frigia I, 2007.

Hierapolis D. Frigia, 1957, 1958.

Humann Carl, Hierapolis, Berlin, 1989.

Mehmet Okunak, Hierapolis Kuzey Nekropolü Anıt Mezar (The Monumental Tomb at the Northern Necropolis of Hierapolis), Yüksek Lisans Tezi (Post-Graduate Thesis), 2005.

Ramsay, W. Anadolu'nun Tarihi Coğrafyası, Translated by Mihri Pektaş. M.E. B. İstanbul, 1960-

Strabon, Coğrafya, Translated by Prof. Dr. Adnan Pekman, İstanbul, 1987.

Tullia Ritti, Hierapolis Fonti Letterarie ed Epigraphice, Roma, 1985.

Verzone Paolo, Hierapolis Di Frigia, Roma, 1978.

1678- 1699 The preliminary report on the ancient city by J. Spoon, G. Wheeler, T. Smith : Reports about the travertines and necropolis

1745 R. Pococke : Describes the theater, the monumental nympheum and the Temple of Apollon

1775 : R. Chandler : Reads various inscriptions of the theatre

1812 : C.R. Cockerell : Describes the Plutonium

1838 : L. De Laborde : Describes the ancient city and its monuments

1839 : Ch. Texier : Illustrates the principle monuments

1898 : C. Humann, C. Cichorius, W. Judeich, F. Winter : The first scientific publication

1957 : Paolo Verzone : The first excavation of the Italian Archaeological Mission. The excavations still continue in Hierapolis leading by Daria De Bernardi Ferrero and Francesco D'Andria.

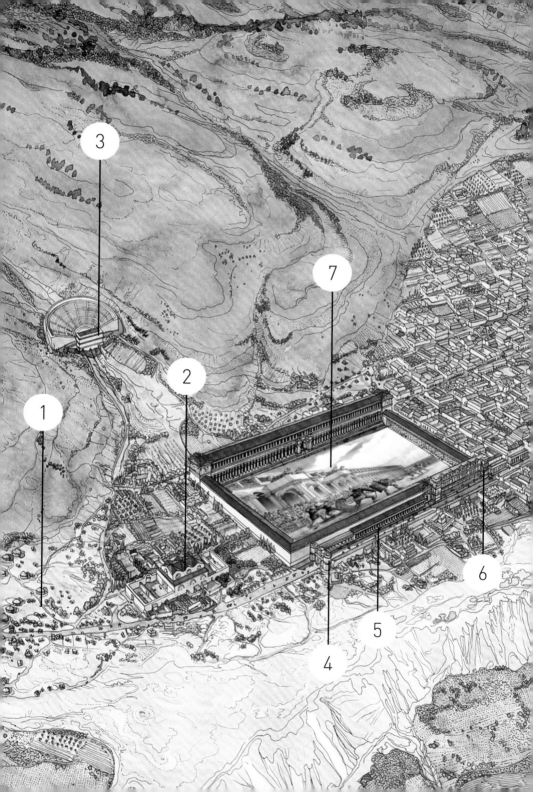

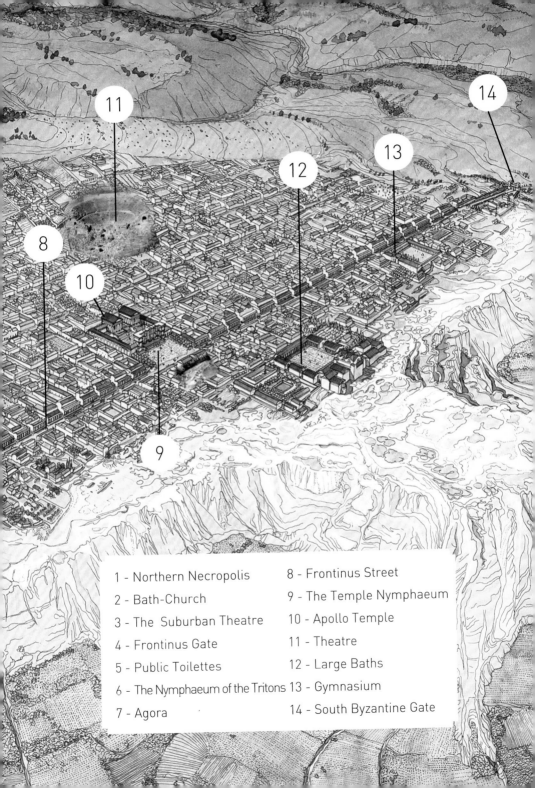

1 - Northern Necropolis

2 - Bath-Church

3 - The Suburban Theatre

4 - Frontinus Gate

5 - Public Toilettes

6 - The Nymphaeum of the Tritons

7 - Agora

8 - Frontinus Street

9 - The Temple Nymphaeum

10 - Apollo Temple

11 - Theatre

12 - Large Baths

13 - Gymnasium

14 - South Byzantine Gate

GLOSSARY

Altar : Place for the sacrifices to the gods

Acropolis : The upper city in which the temples took place

Agora : Market place

Amazons: Legendary women warriors believed to live in the Black Sea Region.

Aphrodite: The goddess of love and beauty

Apollo : The god of music, fine arts, virtue and prophecy

Ariadne : The wife of Dionysos, the god of wine

Artemis : The goddess of fertility and hunting

Asclepios : The god of health and healing

Athena : The goddess of war and the family

Caldarium : The main hot room of the baths

Cavea : The area containing the seats for the audience in the theatre

Cella : The main body of the ancient temples, the most sacred part of a temple in which the sculpture of the god and the goddess took place

Cerberus : The watchman to the door of the Underworld

Chapel : The small part of the church for praying

Cult : The praying temple for gods and goddesses

Demeter : The goddess of the abundance, fertility, earth, crops, agriculture, farming and the nature

Diazoma : The horizontal passage divides the cavea in the theatre

Dionysos : The god of wine and amusement

Eros : The child god. The love begins with the arrows he throws

Frigidarium : The coldest part of a bath

Gaia : The mother earth, a primordial goddess

Giganthomachi : The battle between the gods and the giants

Hades : The lord of the Underworld, the god of the deads

Helios : God of sun

Hera : The wife of the chief god Zeus

Heracles : Half god, represents the power and strenght

Hermes : The god of the passengers, merchants and the herdsmen

Hiera : One of the queens of the Amazons

Horae : Young girl, the goddess of the seasons

Libation : The ceremony of giving sacred water to the gods

Maenad : The female adorants of Dionysos

Magna Mater : The mother goddess

Marsyas: The shepperd who was believed to live between Çine and Yatağan and played flute

Martyr : The person who was dead in name of religion

Men : God of moon

Necropolis : The city of the deads, cemetery

Niche : Hallow having recessed space

Nymphs : The ferries of the water, the forest and the meadow

Octagonal : The eight sided plan

Orchestra : The part of the ancient theatre before the stage

Pan : A mythological figure, half man and half goat

Persephone : The daughter of Demeter, goddess of the nature

Portico : Gallery having columns on both sides

Satyr : The male adorants of the god Dionysos

Tepidarium : The warm water room of the baths